Technology thro

GW00370402

Contents

What is technology?	2
A technologist's approach	3
Raw materials	4
Mechanisms	8
Sound technology	10
Technology for play	12
Cooking	14
Technology in action	16
Thinking together	18
The adult role	20
Making and mending	22
Information technology	23
Other PPA publications	24

Drawings by Tony Benjamin
Cover photographed by Margaret Hanton in Rockingham Playgroup

Produced by CPL Associates 24 Hand Court London WC1V 9JF Tel: 071-831 7690

What is technology?

From their infancy children learn about the physical world, about the objects and resources available in it and the ways these can be used.

As they grow older they begin to be able to draw upon this store of information in order to tackle the practical situations they encounter in their play.

For example a group of children might be pleased to discover that a small empty box will float in the water tray but want to find ways of making their "boat" move across the water. Using their existing knowledge of what makes things move, they might:

- Make a sail
- Blow on the sail, or on the boat itself, either directly or through straws
- Attach the boat to a string and pull it along
- Experiment with ways of creating currents in the water to move the boat along.

As they try out these solutions they might encounter other possible approaches before they decide which solutions work best for them.

This problem solving approach is at the heart of technology. Purposeful play of this kind provides the foundation for later National Curriculum studies in subjects such as science and mathematics as well as technology and design. It also enables children to develop the skills and attitudes they will need in order to function independently in adult life.

The technologist's approach

There are three main elements involved:

The problem

Children encounter a range of problems in their play. An alert adult will help them as necessary to think through the situation and identify where exactly a particular problem lies so that they can focus their resources on tackling it.

The resources

A rich play environment will contain plenty of raw materials for the children to use. More important, children who are in the habit of handling these materials in open-ended play situations where there is no "right" or "wrong" way to do things have a great advantage. They are then able to use whatever is available in a flexible way to achieve the results they want. The development of *lateral thinking* - the ability to use familiar objects and information in new ways - is an essential element in a creative approach to learning.

The approach

Whatever solutions the children think of should be tried out, either by talking them through or by attempting to put them into practice. It will help if children are encouraged to develop the habit of clarifying what they aim to do, then thinking back on it to decide how successful they have been and what changes, if any, need to be made.

> In the course of their problem solving, the children might sometimes make things: something to act as a buffer, for example, to stop the train running off the end of the track. This sort of activity should not be confused with "making" sessions directed by an adult. The point of a technological approach is that the activity arises from a problem perceived by the children and represents their own attempts to solve it.

Raw materials

Children develop the capacity for lateral thinking and a flexible approach to problem solving by having:

- Regular access to a range of materials

- The tools necessary to use them - safety scissors, woodworking equipment (well supervised), pencils, various sorts of glue, string, sticky tape, rubber bands, etc.

- Opportunities to work, with adult support, towards goals set by themselves.

The world abounds with resources for children to use. The following are useful:

NATURAL MATERIALS

Water
Early experiments at the water tray will have helped children to have some understanding of what water is and what it can do. Adults can expand the potential by making accessories available - tubing, funnels, siphons, sprinklers - and discussing their use with the children.

Sand
Play at the sand tray and on the beach will have introduced children to the properties of sand: the fact that it will pour when dry, yet can still support upright any objects pushed into it; its heaviness when wet; the way it will hold a shape when damp.

Metal
Most children will have encountered metal in the form of metal objects such as nails and tin lids. They will have learned about its strength and hardness, the fact that it holds its shape under pressure and perhaps also about the way it can be polished to shine and reflect, and the sounds it can make when struck.

Wood
In the form of blocks, jigsaws and other wooden playthings as well as in trees, twigs and plants, wood will be familiar to most children. They will know how it feels, how strong it is and also perhaps how it can be sanded smooth, how it floats and how pieces of wood can be nailed together. The opportunity, well supervised, to use saws and screwdrivers can extend children's understanding of wood and of what it can do.

Clay/dough
Children who have had access to these basic materials from an early age will be accustomed to handling them and will know some of the things they can do, such as holding a shape, fitting into a mould, baking hard, accepting imprints, weighting things down or sticking things together.

MANUFACTURED MATERIALS

Paper
If this has been regularly available, not just for "painting a picture" but to explore in other ways, children will be aware that paper can be cut and torn, squashed into balls and folded into shapes; that it will float for a while when dry and sink when soaked. Some children might also have played with wet paper and know something about what can be done with papier mâché.

Cardboard
Children's experience of this material will probably include the light card of cereal packets, which can be glued and coloured like paper while being stiffer than paper, and the endless usefulness of cardboard boxes - for building with, cutting up, putting things in, jumping over and sticking things on.

Textiles
All children know something about manufactured fabrics through their experience of their own clothing and the furnishings in their groups and homes. If they have been given opportunities to discuss and explore a range of fabrics they will be aware that some are much thicker and stronger than others; that their textures vary; that some are stretchy; that they often have printed patterns or pictures which can be cut out and used separately; that woven fabrics can be frayed out into a fringe; that fabric with holes or a loose weave can be used as a sieve.

Plastics
Plastic sheeting in any form (bags, carriers, clingfilm etc) should be used only under adult supervision. However, children of playgroup age will know something about plastic and will of course be familiar with plastic containers. Children are especially interested in the fact that even the thin, transparent plastic of (eg) sandwich bags will hold water.

Discarded/found materials
A rich and varied assortment, stored in a way which allows both adults and children to know what there is and where to find it, is invaluable. Materials which are no longer being used for their

original purpose leave children free to use them in whatever way suits their own needs and intentions. Materials to provide include: corks, lids and bottle caps (small ones not to be available to children young or immature enough to put them in their mouths/noses), scraps of lace, tweed, velvet and sequinned fabric, wooden offcuts, moulded packaging (eg from chocolate boxes), conkers, sea shells, washed eggshells, buttons, newspaper, boxes, tubes and cartons of assorted shapes and sizes.

One of the "tools" children will most commonly use in connection with all these materials is glue. Encourage them to recognise the differing kinds of glue which are available in the playgroup. They will learn through experiment and discussion which kinds of adhesive work best in particular situations; that a light paste is excellent for tissue paper, for example, but you need a heavy PVA glue to stick leaves on fabric.

Mechanisms

Children are fascinated by things that work, and the way they work. Given the right equipment and the necessary adult support, this natural interest forms the basis of an understanding of many simple mechanisms.

Babies and toddlers are often supplied with "activity boards", bought or homemade, which enable them to explore hinges, bolts, switches etc. Older children need opportunities to see these devices in use and to understand their purpose.

Ready made help

Children learn a lot by improvising their own solutions to problems but there are many pieces of equipment which can help them to understand, as they play and explore, the principles underlying mechanisms.

Construction sets such as Lego and Meccano can be extended to include gears. Some children are fascinated by the way these interlock and turn one another. It is worthwhile keeping a separate, smaller box within the big Lego container to hold gears, lights, wheels, axles, joints and other special small pieces.

Kits which allow toy vehicles etc to be taken apart and reassembled let children look at their component parts. It is especially useful to buy kits which allow children to see clearly the relationship between wheels and axles so that they begin to understand why circles glued to their model of a car, although they look like wheels, will not turn round.

Interlocking train/road tracks are also useful, especially if there are sufficient pieces and accessories for some children to be able to design tracks for a specific purpose: to get the produce from the model farm to the people in the dolls' house or to loop round an obstacle or cross a "river". For younger children, getting the two ends of the track to meet in a circle is a design challenge in itself.

The real world

Children can learn from grown-up equipment too. Particularly fascinating to some children are things which are designed to fold up. Such children can be helped to extend their interest by looking at deckchairs, umbrellas, fans, pack flat storage materials (eg a range of fold-up/slot together wine racks) and the elaborate "paper engineering" in some children's books and greetings cards. Given the right materials and support, these children might be interested to try creating simple "lift the flap" pictures for themselves.

The playgroup itself probably owns mechanisms which can be used to extend children's understanding. It is easy to forget that equipment which is routine for adults may be new and fascinating to small children. The hinged flap which turns the playhouse into a shop, or the simple pulley which keeps all the soft toys in a net under the ceiling of the storage cupboard, are sources of interest and learning and the adults in a good playgroup are alert to seize the opportunities.

Give the appropriate tools many children learn a lot from the chance to dismantle, for example, an old telephone or record-player. An adult must check in advance that the children will not encounter parts which are sharp or otherwise dangerous and the children themselves must clearly understand that this activity is strictly for disused, disconnected items.

Sound technology

Most children like to make a noise! They can be encouraged to think about how sounds are made and to make "instruments" of their own - which might or might not resemble conventional ones.

Twanging

Any tightly stretched cord gives out a sound when it is plucked. Many children will already know how to make a tiny "guitar" by stretching elastic bands over an open topped box such as a matchbox. Let them experiment with other applications of the same principle: nylon string stretched tightly between the legs of an upturned chair/table, for example, or a length of elastic round a big cardboard carton or biscuit tin.

Banging

Percussion does not have to be a noisy affair. Children can progress from banging on saucepans and tin drums to trying out a wider range of sounds. They can bang with wooden or metal strikers - or tights/stockings with knots in the end - on wooden, cardboard or plastic objects, either solid or hollow ones.

Shaking

The homemade maracas used in most playgroups as rhythm makers have the potential for many variations. If there are plenty of materials to use, together with adult support, children will be able to make different sorts of sounds by trying containers of various sizes and substances, each with a number of different fillings: large and small items; hard and soft ones, including conkers, rice grains, buttons, sand, cotton wool balls and wood shavings.

Rubbing

Once children discover that surfaces with different textures make different noises when rubbed against each other, they can try out a range of surfaces to find out which sounds they prefer. They might experiment with sandpaper, corded fabric stretched over building blocks, corrugated card, notched wood, crepe paper or pieces of bark.

Chiming

Objects suspended from one end make a quite different noise when struck. Graduated lengths of metal tubing hanging from a bar can create a scale, but the children can do their own experiments with a few long nails, giant metal paperclips or old spoons and forks, with a coathanger to dangle them from.

Rustling

Once children have been helped to be alert to all the possibilities for soundmaking, they will not stop at the samples listed above. From the sound of water swishing in a bottle to the rustling of foil milk bottle tops in a paper bag, the potential is endless.

In the course of their play, ir
materials and adult encour
of problems and will work t

Faced with the challenge of creating an indoor
"garden" on a tray, children will need to seek
materials to represent trees and flowers and
some means of keeping these upright. They
might even fill their tray with water and look for
something which can serve as an island. It will
have to be something which will hold its shape
and can have "houses" and/or "vegetation"
stuck on/in it, but it cannot be made of a
substance which will wash away in the water.

Children playing ir
out how to keep w
prevent a tunnel t
cars which are to

PR
SC

An imaginary fire in the dolls' house
might require the assistance of a the
toy fire engine.

*What happens if the ladders are not
long enough to reach the upper
windows where the dolls are?*

*Is there some way the ladder can be
extended?*

How else might the dolls get down?

Having been given a large ca
freezer was delivered, the c
using the end flaps as "doo
able to fasten their "doors"
they ask the playleader for s
idea because they want the
opened. They decide that a
and start to glue it onto one
they fix it in place but then
When they are in danger of t
can think of no means of a
suggests fixing to the other
over the knob. The children
are stored to find somethin
with some ribbon, a length
now have to choose the mo
attaching it to the "door"....

for play

oup environment rich in raw
, children will meet a range
1em.

nay need to work
moat, or how to
in on top of the
gh it.

EM
G

Children playing a "chase" game are trying to make one of the sit and ride cars look more like a police car. They have made a "blue light" by painting an inverted paper cup and are now trying to find a way of fixing it onto the car. They discover that glue will not work and one child suggests attaching the cup to the back of the car with sticky tape. Another child protests that the light should go "high up" so they decide to mount the cup on a cardboard carton. They do so quite successfully but they then have to decide how to secure the cardboard carton to the car....

arton in which a commercial
e playing in it as a "house"
decide that they want to be
em swinging open. At first
y tape but they discard this
be able to be closed *and*
otton reel looks like a knob
ors". With a little adult help
d a way to make it "work".
disheartened because they
what they want, the adult
oop which can be dropped
e place where the materials
a loop. They come back
and a rubber band. They
material and find a way of

If the smallest doll keeps slipping off its chair at the "tea party", what can the children do about it? *Might they adapt the chair so that it holds the doll more securely? Or make some sort of harness? Or devise an alternative seat?*

Cooking

Cookery may not seem a very technological activity but children engaged in *food preparation are learning to:

Use tools

Some of the tools used in cooking are too dangerous for young children but there are many simple tools they can learn to use and they can then also select the one most appropriate for the job in hand. Children can be introduced to:

Blunt knives - for spreading

Rolling pins - for rolling pastry and also for making crumbs by banging biscuits inside a bag

Balloon whisks/forks - for mixing milkshakes, beating eggs

Graters - for cheese, carrots etc. (A rotary grater with a handle is easier for small children to use and avoids damage to fingers.)

Cutters - in a range of shapes and sizes.

Develop techniques

■ As adults help them to seal currants inside the pastry for Eccles cakes, wrap the pastry around the filling for samosas or create a convex pastry shape to hold the jam inside a jam tart, children are learning different approaches to the same problem.

■ Making sandwiches, children will discover that dry fillings need a little margarine on the bread to hold them in place – and what happens if the filling is not evenly spread across the sandwich.

Make sure that hands and surfaces are clean and that the food is enjoyed as soon as possible after preparation.

■ Children icing and decorating biscuits are learning the necessary practical skills of spreading and sprinkling and will also begin to judge what kind of decorations stick most successfully to the icing and how quickly they need to be applied before the icing dries.

Manipulate materials

Rolling chapattis or pastry and adding flour or water if necessary, mixing cake ingredients together, arranging the fillings on the sandwich, cleaning and cutting up a range of vegetables to make soup, children are not just developing practical skills, useful though these are. They are also using techniques they have already acquired in other areas in order to deal with new situations.

This aspect of technology, like all others, should be available to *all* children. It is especially important not to allow children's full participation to be limited by assumptions about what activities are "suitable" for boys or girls. It might be necessary for the adults actively to encourage boys to cook - and girls to take part in some of the activities suggested in other chapters.

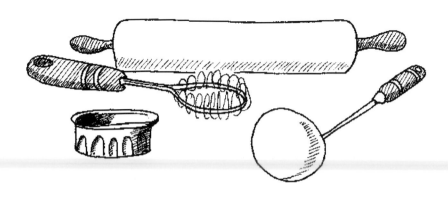

Technology in action

Sometimes the opportunity arises to improvise a piece of play equipment from the materials available in the playgroup. If the children are involved in this, they can be helped to join in the decision making and problem solving involved and may well come up with ideas of their own.

Skittles

These are easy to make from empty squash bottles, but when they are empty they fall over too readily. Children can be encouraged to think about the reasons for this, about the ideal weight for skittles and the best way of weighting them (sand?...water?... clay?...pebbles?...) *Is a small quantity of something very heavy better or worse than a larger quantity of something lighter?*

Jewellery

If the "pirates" need a treasure chest or the people "dressing up to go out" in the home play area want something special to wear, the children can be encouraged to think about what could be used to create "jewels": necklaces, bracelets, brooches* and earrings. This is where well sorted materials, readily accessible to the children, are important. If they know where to find labelled storage boxes (lidded ice cream tubs are ideal) containing milk bottle tops, crushed coloured eggshell, pasta shapes past their sell-by date and other small, bright things then they have a range of appropriate materials to work with and can plan accordingly.

It is useful too if the adults in the group have a "secret store" of special equipment such as gold paint, glitter, etc to be brought out as necessary to help with such projects.

> *These are fun to make and need not involve pins: double sided sticky tape or a piece of Velcro on the back will hold them in place on most dressing-up clothes.*

Boats

From tin trays to corks and walnut shells, children can explore a wide range of things which will float and can then consider what kind of boat they want to make and what other materials and techniques to use. They might want to find a way of making a mast stand up or they might be more concerned to create/adapt a boat for a specific purpose: to carry "containers" made of boxes if they have seen container ships while on holiday, or perhaps to accommodate animals on a "Noah's Ark".

Buildings

Play with model aeroplanes or the self assembly train track might create the need for an airport or railway station. Different children will have different problems to solve because each will contribute according to his/her own experience. One child might want to make a wind sock and will have to search for paper, paint or fabric of the right colour and then find a way of fixing it to an upright and getting the finished model to stand up. Another child might have been excited by going over the station footbridge above the trains and want to try to fold a sheet of paper to make it into "steps".

> When buying new materials for the playgroup, keep in mind the advantages of open-ended equipment that the children can use to adapt and transform their own play environment. Lengths of fabric (eg old curtains), large cartons, cushions and lightweight planking can provide food for children's imaginations.

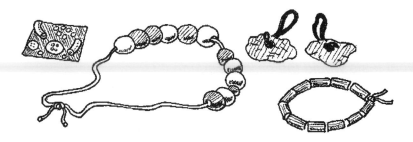

Thinking together

Technology does not consist only of making things. It also involves *thinking through* problems and situations and bringing all available resources to bear upon them.

In this, children are not there just to be instructed by adults about "how to do it". On the contrary, children are often better at it than adults. They are less restricted than we are by pre-conceived ideas about how things "ought" to be done and are therefore sometimes more flexible in their thinking.

Discussing problems and projects together in a group is an ideal way to foster problem solving skills:

- Everyone can help, but nobody is under any pressure to succeed individually.

- All children can participate on equal terms, including those with physical disabilities.

- Discussion in a group enables children to pool their suggestions. As well as being more fun, this often releases more ideas as one prompts another.

There are several ways of tackling problems together:

Talk about stories
Many children's stories pose problems or challenges for the characters in them; invite the children to come up with solutions of their own. In *The Wolf and the Seven Little Kids*, for example, the seven kids try to devise tests to find out whether it is their mother or the wolf knocking at the door.

What tests would the children suggest?

How could they trick the wolf?

Talk about measurement

Discussing different ways of doing the same thing can help children realise that alternative approaches are possible and that if one method fails they can try another. If an activity needs to be timed for example - perhaps when children are taking turns with a popular piece of equipment - let the children suggest ways of doing so. They might think of a stopwatch, a wristwatch alarm, a kitchen timer or "how long it takes to count to ten". If they become interested in systems of measurement, they could be introduced to an eggtimer, a sundial, or even a simple candle clock.

Talk about shared activities

Projects which are being approached as a group can be greatly enriched by talking them through together. If the plan is to make a book for example - a collection of the children's pictures, a record of the latest group outing or a "feely" book of interesting textures - the children can discuss how books are made, how the pages can be joined together and how the cover should go on. If a farm or zoo is to be created to house the plastic animals, the group can discuss in advance what kind of accommodation is needed for different animals and what requirements need to be met - the best size, for example, the layout, feeding equipment and specific needs such as trees to swing from or water to swim in.

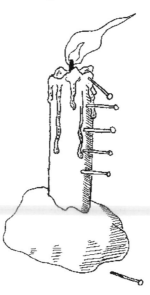

The adult role

The adult role in technological education at any age or stage is a demanding one, but very rewarding. Rather than doing things on children's behalf or giving instructions on how to achieve results the adult way, the adults in playgroup will :

Provide resources

A wide range of raw materials, classified and stored in a way which gives ready access to them, enables children to know the possibilities and to draw on them to meet their particular needs. If children cannot take things directly from the place where they are stored, a small table or collapsible tea trolley can hold the boxes containing (eg) corks, leaves, stiff card, fabric scraps, lids and caps, paper etc.

Assist with tools

Some tools, such as staplers, must remain in possession of the adults, but children need to know about them so that they can ask for them if necessary. Other tools, such as scissors which really cut, should be readily available. Suitable scissors should also be available for left handed children. Woodworking tools should be of good quality and well supervised. Give time to introducing children to their use so that they come to know the advantages, for example, of using a clamp or vice for jobs which need both hands free.

A book about tools is a useful addition to the book corner. *Read about tools* by Henry Pluckrose (Franklin Watts - £6.50) is aimed at young children and contains good clear photographs.

Make things possible

Children will not learn to think for themselves if they are over directed, but they must not be left to flounder. If children have made a "parking sign" for their road layout, but cannot make it stand up, the adult might help them to think through a number of ways of making things stand upright: fastening them to an existing upright; giving them a broad, heavy base by sticking them into a piece of clay/plasticine; suspending them from above; creating a base by making slits in two pieces of flat wood/card and slotting them together at right angles to one another. The children then have a range of techniques to choose from, on this and future occasions.

Involve children in the life of the group

If you are moving over to a "coffee bar" system of serving a drink and snack but need a way of checking who has had their snack and who has not, invite the children to think of solutions. They might suggest ways of labelling food and drinks, of "signing" for snacks taken, or vouchers/tokens to exchange for a drink - or they might come up with something entirely different.

If the storage boxes, lids and contents get muddled, think together as a group about the different kinds of labels and labelling systems. *(Lids covered to match boxes? Pictures of contents on boxes and lids? Jigsaw pieces marked on the reverse with the colour of the box they belong in? Shelves marked with the colour/ pattern of the boxes which belong there?)*

Create links

Help children to understand that the same technique can serve different purposes. For example, many children enjoy folding paper and like making cut out "snowflakes" from tissue paper. The folding theme can be extended to show that folding paper can create a "concertina" - for a fan, for stairs in the dolls' house or for useful troughs in which to arrange beads for threading; the folding can also create repeating patterns such as rows of figures - or, of course, paper decorations for parties.

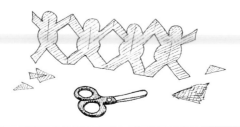

Making and mending

Too much of the life of a playgroup is often hidden from the children. It can be very useful to create a space in which adults who are helping the group by making or repairing playgroup equipment can, if they are willing and the task is suitable, come in and do the work in view of the children. Children are always interested to see adults working. As they stand and watch, ask questions or just have a look in passing, they become aware of:

■ How adults use skills and resources and tackle problems

■ A range of materials and the uses to which they can be put: the clear plastic which reinforces books; the scrap of stretchy fabric which makes leggings for the dolls; the waterproof material which makes a lift-off cover for the clay table - and the elastic which creates a snug fit at its corners

■ The tools which make jobs easier: sewing and knitting needles, which will be new to some children, as well as a lightweight sewing machine if possible; the ratchet screwdriver which repairs the playhouse; the kit for putting drawstring eyelets in the bag in which the train lines are to be stored; the manual typewriter which produces notices for the playgroup notice board.

Craft activities which are not genuinely within the range of pre-school children can still be a source of ideas and interest for them if an adult comes into the playgroup to make, for example, decorations for a special event.

Information technology

Electronic methods of compiling, storing and retrieving information are part of today's world and few of our pre-school children will grow up without encountering computers in some form.

If your children do not have access to a computer but you want to familiarise them with the general approach, do not waste money on the "just like mummy's/daddy's" toys which simulate the appearance of a computer screen and keyboard without calling on similar skills or routines. Look instead for simple electronic toys which have to be *programmed* (ie given a sequence of clear instructions in a particular order) to make them work.

In more general terms, all the activities described in this book, because they foster a rational, enquiring, flexible approach to problems of all kinds, form an ideal preparation for later encounters with electronic equipment.

If you have a computer, choose the software carefully. Many software packages for young children claim to be "educational". *Ignore such claims and make your own judgement.* Look for genuinely interactive material in which the children's responses are built on, enabling them to progress at their own pace. This is not the same as programmes which do not *teach* but merely *test* existing knowledge by giving children's answers the electronic equivalent of a tick or a cross.

With well chosen software, computers can be useful:

■ To give children confidence in a medium they will encounter later

■ To offer children with disabilities opportunities for the excitement and rapid positive feedback they might sometimes lack.

Other PPA publications you might find useful

PPA Guidelines
Good Practice for Sessional Playgroups
Good Practice for Full Daycare Playgroups
Good Practice for Parent and Toddler Playgroups

PPA Play Activities
Glueing
Sand and Water
Make Believe Play
Play and Dough

Learn Through Play
Language Through Play
Science Through Play
Maths Through Play
Shapes and Colours Through Play

PPA Training
PPA Diploma in Playgroup Practice - course content

Starting a Playgroup (A4 pack)
What Children Learn in Playgroup
The Playgroup Session
Running a Parent and Toddler Playgroup
Accident Prevention and First Aid
Playgroup Register
Playgroup Account Book
Playgroup Accident and Incident Book
Learn Through Play display cards
Equal Chances

A complete list of PPA publications and promotional goods is available for SAE from: PPA National Centre, 61-63 Kings Cross Road, London WC1X 9LL.